ALCOHOL & CANCER

Copyright

Dedication

This book is dedicated to the relentless pursuit of knowledge, innovation, and professional excellence. To the mentors whose guidance has been an invaluable compass, steering through the complexities of the subject matter. To colleagues, whose collaborative spirit has enriched the journey of research and creation.

May this work contribute to the ongoing discourse in our field and inspire future endeavors aimed at advancing our understanding and practices.

With gratitude,

DR.MARC REGAN hii

Table Of Content

Introduction

The intricate relationship between alcohol consumption and health has long been a subject of study, particularly regarding its impact on cardiovascular health. Moderation, defined as no more than 2 drinks per day for women and a maximum of 3 drinks per day for men, is often associated with low-risk drinking and potential cardiovascular benefits.

However, the dual nature of alcohol is evident, as its consumption has been linked to detrimental effects, notably an increased risk of specific illnesses and elevated mortality rates. The International Agency for Research on Cancer (IARC) recognized alcohol as a risk factor for various cancers as early as 1988, marking a pivotal moment in understanding its implications on health.

In 2017, the Canadian Cancer Society reported a significant impact of cancer related to alcohol, with 10, 310 new cases (5% of total) and 3, 636 fatalities (4. 5% of total) attributed to this risk. The magnitude of cancer risk associated with alcohol consumption varies depending on the type and amount of alcohol consumed.

This report delves into the biological pathways activated by alcohol, shedding light on how it influences cancer risk. Exploring different risk variables, the association between drinking and cancer is thoroughly examined. The final section addresses preventive measures, highlighting various strategies to reduce cancer risk.

Understanding cancer risk is a nuanced process, influenced by individual profiles and behaviors. This report aims to contribute to the comprehensive discourse surrounding alcohol consumption and its intricate relationship with cancer development and prevention.

The relationship between alcohol consumption and cancer has been a subject of increasing concern and study in the field of public health. While moderate alcohol consumption has been associated with certain potential health benefits, the evidence linking alcohol to an increased risk of various cancers has become a significant focus of research.

Alcohol, a widely consumed psychoactive substance, plays a complex role in the development of cancer. The intricate interplay between genetic factors, drinking patterns, and specific types of cancer has led researchers to delve deeper into understanding the mechanisms through which alcohol may contribute to oncogenesis.

This introduction aims to explore the current scientific understanding of the connection between alcohol and cancer, examining the key factors influencing this relationship, and highlighting the importance of informed public health decisions regarding alcohol consumption.

Chapter 1: Definition Of Alcohol

Alcohol, a molecule of complex repute, is not confined to the realms of celebratory toasts but extends its presence into a myriad of consumables and products. This intricate compound can be found in alcoholic beverages such as beer, wine, and liquor, weaving its way into the fabric of various medications, mouthwashes, home goods, and even the fragrant allure of essential oils extracted from specific plants.

1. Origins and Production:

At its core, alcohol, particularly the type found in alcoholic beverages, is ethyl alcohol or ethanol. The genesis of ethanol lies in the chemical dance of fermentation.

This intricate process utilizes yeast and sugar, transforming these basic components into the intoxicating elixir that has been a part of human culture for centuries.

2. Ubiquity Beyond Drinks:

The ubiquity of alcohol extends far beyond the glass. Medications, serving as carriers for therapeutic compounds, may contain ethanol. Mouthwashes utilize its antiseptic properties, home goods benefit from its solvent characteristics, and essential oils capture its aromatic essence to provide scents derived from the bounty of nature.

3. Varieties of Alcohol:

The term "alcohol" is a broad classification encompassing various types. However, when referring to the alcohol used in the crafting of alcoholic beverages, it is specifically denoted as ethyl alcohol or ethanol. This distinction is crucial in understanding its unique role in the world of libations.

4. The Alchemy of Fermentation:

The journey of alcohol production commences with the intricate alchemy of fermentation. Yeast, acting as the catalyst, engages with sugars and starches to orchestrate a transformation. Through this chemical symphony, alcohol emerges as a product of the microbial and biochemical ballet.

5. Intoxicating Substance - Ethanol:

Beer, wine, and liquor, those venerable companions of conviviality, all share a common denominator — the intoxicating substance known as ethanol. This ethereal elixir, born from the fermentation of yeast, sugars, and starches, imbues these beverages with the characteristic allure that has echoed through history.

In essence, the presence and production of alcohol, particularly ethanol, constitute a rich tapestry woven through the realms of both celebration and utility. From the frothy realms of beer to the nuanced notes of wine and the potent embrace of spirits, ethanol's journey from yeast and sugar to intoxicating libation is a tale that spans cultures, traditions, and scientific intricacies.

Types Of Alcohol

Exploring Alcohol Types:

1. Ethyl Alcohol (Ethanol):

The cornerstone of beer, wine, and spirits, ethanol is the magical element that induces the sensation of intoxication. In the realm of secondary alcohols, methanol, isopropanol, and ethanol are prominent members. Notably, only ethyl alcohol is deemed safe for human consumption, with its counterparts finding utility in cleaning and manufacturing. Isopropanol or methanol use is cautioned due to their potential risks, including lethality.

2. Isopropyl Alcohol:

Known as rubbing alcohol, isopropyl alcohol takes center stage in sterilization. Its applications span cleaning and sanitizing instruments, surfaces, and even human skin. This versatile alcohol is present in cosmetics, lotions, and various cleaning products.

3. Methyl Alcohol:

Often referred to as wood alcohol, methyl alcohol finds its niche in manufacturing. Its byproducts contribute to the creation of diverse goods, from plastics to explosives. With applications like paint remover and antifreeze, this alcohol type serves multifaceted roles. It also prevents freezing in fuels and can fuel both cars and boats.

4. Ethyl Alcohol (Ethanol) - Recreational and Risks:

The ancient practice of fermenting sugars, yeast, and starches gives birth to ethanol or grain alcohol. While historically embraced for recreational purposes due to its mood-altering effects, it's crucial to note that ethanol, in excess, poses health risks. Chronic consumption can lead to damage to vital organs, including the liver, kidneys, and brain. Ethanol misuse may result in a central nervous system disorder, impaired judgment, coordination, and addiction.

5. Distilled and Undistilled Alcohol:

Measurement of alcohol in fermented beverages involves terms like alcohol by volume (ABV) and alcohol proof. Distilled drinks, such as liquors and spirits, have higher alcohol proof and more alcohol by volume compared to non-distilled beverages.

Categories of Alcoholic Drinks by Alcohol Content:

1. Undistilled Drinks:

Beer, a globally consumed beverage, typically ranges from 2. 5% to 15% ABV. Wine, with origins dating back over 9, 000 years, undergoes fermentation of crushed grapes and can be categorized into red, white, rosé, sparkling, and fortified. Cider, mead, and sake, each with distinct production processes, contribute to the diverse world of undistilled drinks.

2. Distilled Drinks (Liquors and Spirits):

The world of distilled drinks introduces various potent libations. Gin, brandy, whiskey, rum, tequila, vodka, and absinthe are among the lineup. Each undergoes a unique distillation process, resulting in distinctive flavors and alcohol content ranging from 35% to 90% ABV.

In essence, the tapestry of alcohol is woven with threads of variety, from the recreational allure of fermented beverages to the potent and diverse realm of distilled spirits. Understanding the types and applications of alcohol provides insights into both cultural practices and the potential risks associated with consumption.

Chapter 2: Is Alcohol A Drug

It is categorized as a depressant, which means that it slows down
essential processes, causing slurred speech, shaky movement,
foggy perceptions, and a delayed response time.

When it comes to how it affects the mind, it's easiest to view
of it as a substance that impairs one's capacity for reason and
clouds their judgment.

Despite being a depressant, the sort of effect depends on how
much alcohol is consumed. The majority of drinkers do so to feel more energized, such as when they "loosen up" with a beer or glass of wine. But when someone consumes more alcohol than their body can tolerate, they start to feel depressed.

They start to experience coordination and control issues or feel
"dumb."

An excessive intake of alcohol has much more potent depressive effects (inability to feel pain, toxicity where the body vomits the poison, and finally unconsciousness or, worse, coma or death from severe toxic overdose). How much and how soon
is consumed affects these effects.

There are various types of alcohol. The sole type of alcohol used in beverages is ethanol (ethanol), which is created when grains and fruits are fermented. Alcohol is produced through fermentation, a chemical process, in which yeast reacts with
specific food materials.

ALCOHOL CONTENT

Beer and wine are examples of fermented beverages that

range in alcohol content from 2% to 20%.
Alcohol content
ranges from 40% to 50% or more in distilled beverages, or liquor.

For each, the typical alcohol content is:
Beer has an alcohol content of 2-6%.
4-8% alcohol content in cider
8–20% alcohol by volume in wine
40% tequila alcohol
40% or more alcohol in rum
40% or more alcohol is in brandy.
Gin contains 40–47% alcohol.
Whiskey contains 40–50% alcohol.
vodka with 40–50% alcohol
Liqueurs contain 15–60% alcohol.

Does Alcohol Really Cause Cancer

Alcohol consumption is strongly linked to the development of several cancers, including oropharynx, larynx, esophagus, liver, colon, rectum, breast cancer, and potentially others like pancreas, prostate, and skin cancer. The evidence supporting these connections is robust.

The level of risk is influenced by the quantity of alcohol consumed. Men exceeding four alcoholic drinks per day and women surpassing three face a heightened risk. It's essential to acknowledge that attributing cancer solely to alcohol oversimplifies the intricate nature of these diseases. Numerous factors contribute, and only a small percentage of individuals who consume alcohol will actually develop one of these cancers as a direct result of their alcohol consumption.

Indeed, acknowledging the complexity is crucial for a nuanced perspective on the intricate relationship between alcohol consumption and cancer risk.

This involves considering various factors such as individual health, genetic predispositions, and lifestyle choices. Such nuanced understanding is essential for informed decision-making, public health strategies, and fostering awareness of the multifaceted nature of alcohol-related cancer risks.

Chapter 3: New Genetic Study Confirms That Alcohol Is A Direct Cause Of Cancer

New evidence from an extensive genetic investigation done
by Oxford Population Health supports the notion that alcohol
causes cancer directly.

Over 400,000 of the 3 million deaths associated with alcohol
each year in the world are cancer-related.

Understanding how alcohol influences disease risks in various populations is urgently needed, especially in fast growing
nations like China where alcohol consumption is on the rise.

Alcohol is clearly a primary cause of cancers of the head, neck, oesophagus, liver, colon, and breast, according to evidence from Western nations. But it has been challenging to determine if alcohol promotes cancer directly or if it is connected to potential confounding variables (such smoking and food) that could lead to skewed results. A connection between alcohol and other cancers, such as stomach and lung cancer, is also unknown.

By looking into gene variants linked to lower alcohol use in Asian populations, researchers from Oxford Population Health, Peking University, and the Chinese Academy of Medical Sciences, Beijing, took a genomic approach to addressing these

unanswered questions. Today, the findings were released in the
International Journal of Cancer.
Because they have an unpleasant "flushing" impact, two
common genetic variations (alleles) in Chinese and other East
Asian populations impair alcohol tolerance and are highly
related with lower alcohol intake.

Both of these mutations
impair the ability of enzymes involved in alcohol detoxification,
which leads to an accumulation of the dangerous chemical
acetaldehyde, a Group I carcinogen, in the blood.

The gene for the enzyme aldehyde dehydrogenase 2 has a
loss-of-function mutation as the first mutation (ALDH2).

The second mutation increases alcohol dehydrogenase 1B's activity (ADH1B).

Both are prevalent in East Asians but uncommon in people of European descent.
These genes can be used as a proxy for alcohol intake to determine how alcohol consumption influences disease risks because they are assigned at birth and are unaffected by other lifestyle factors (such as smoking).

The study team determined the frequency of the low-alcohol tolerance alleles for ALDH2 and ADH1B using DNA samples from nearly 150,000 participants (roughly 60,000 men and 90,000 women) in the China Kadoorie Biobank project. The

information was paired with questionnaires regarding drinking
behaviors that individuals had to answer both at recruiting and
at later follow-up visits. By connecting the participants' data
to mortality and health insurance databases, the subjects were followed for a median of 11 years. In China, women don't often consume alcohol, therefore the
major analysis concentrated on men, of whom a third routinely
consumed alcohol (most weeks in the past year).

Key results:
Low-alcohol toleration allele frequency in the Chinese research population was 21% for ALDH2 and 69% for ADH1B (as
opposed to 0.01% and 4% in populations of European ancestry).
The low-alcohol tolerance alleles in men were significantly
associated with lower alcohol use, including frequency of

drinking and mean intake.
Approximately 4,500 (7.4%) of the men had cancer during
the follow-up period.

Men who carried one or more of the ADH1B low-alcohol
tolerance alleles had between 13-25% decreased risks for
oesophageal, head, and neck cancers as well as other alcoholrelated cancers.

Overall, men who had two copies of ALDH2's low-alcohol
tolerance allele drank very little alcohol and had a 14% lower
chance of getting any type of cancer as well as a 31% lower risk
of getting malignancies that have previously been associated
with alcohol (cancers of the head and neck; oesophagus, colon,
rectum and liver).

Despite having one copy of the low-alcohol tolerance allele
for ALDH2, men who habitually drank had significantly increased chances of oesophageal and head and neck cancer.

There was no general correlation between having one copy
of the ALDH2 low-alcohol tolerance allele and an increased
risk of cancer in non- or infrequent drinkers.

When the data were corrected for other cancer risk factors
such smoking, nutrition, physical activity, body mass, and family history of cancer, the conclusions remained the same.

These low-alcohol tolerance alleles were not linked to an
elevated risk of cancer in women (only 2% of whom drank
frequently), suggesting that the lower risks for males who

carried these gene variants were a direct result of men's lower
alcohol use.

The significantly higher risks found in males who continued to drink regularly and carried the low-alcohol tolerance ALDH2 gene mutation shows that higher levels of acetaldehyde buildup may directly enhance cancer risk.

Chapter 4: Definition Of Cancer

Cancer is a condition characterized by the uncontrolled growth and spread of cells within the body. It can originate in any of the trillions of cells that compose the human body. Normally, cells undergo a regulated process of growth and multiplication to replace old or damaged cells. However, when this process malfunctions, damaged or abnormal cells can proliferate, forming masses of tissue known as tumors.

Tumors can be either benign or malignant. Benign tumors typically remain localized and do not invade neighboring tissues. They often do not pose a significant threat and may not require extensive treatment. On the other hand, malignant tumors, also known as cancerous tumors, have the potential to metastasize. This means they can spread to distant parts of the body, invading nearby tissues and forming new tumors.

Malignant tumors are a serious concern, as they can affect the normal functioning of organs and systems. Unlike benign tumors, malignant tumors can recur even after removal, making them more challenging to manage. While some cancers, such as blood malignancies like leukemia, may not form solid tumors, many other types of cancer are characterized by the development of these abnormal masses.

It's important to note that benign tumors, despite not being cancerous, can still cause complications, especially if they grow large or occur in critical areas like the brain.

How Does Cancer Develop

Cancer is indeed a genetic disease. Genetic alterations or mutations in the genes that regulate cell growth and division can lead to uncontrolled cell growth and which is a hallmark of cancer. These genetic alterations can occur due to various factors.

One source of genetic alterations is mistakes that happen during the normal process of cell division. When cells divide and their DNA is replicated and sometimes errors or mutations can occur in the DNA sequence. These mutations can affect the genes that control cell growth and division to abnormal cell behavior and the development of cancer.

Additionally and exposure to certain environmental factors can also cause genetic alterations that contribute to cancer development. For example and exposure to carcinogens such as those found in tobacco smoke or UV radiation from the sun can lead to DNA damage and mutations in the genes involved in cell growth and division.

It's important to note that not all genetic mutations or DNA damage will result in cancer. Our bodies havc mcchanisms in place to repair or eliminate cells with damaged DNA. However and as we age and the body's ability to repair DNA damage may decline and increasing the likelihood of cancer development.

Furthermore and each person's cancer is unique in terms of the genetic mutations present. Different individuals may have different genetic alterations in their cancer cells and even within the same tumor and different cells may have different genetic alterations. This genetic heterogeneity makes cancer a complex and challenging disease to treat effectively.

Understanding the genetic alterations that drive cancer development is crucial for developing targeted therapies and personalized treatment approaches in cancer care.

Cause Of Cancer

Changes (mutations) to the DNA within cells are what lead
to cancer. A cell's DNA is organized into numerous distinct
genes, each of which carries a set of instructions directing
the cell's performance of certain tasks as well as its growth
and division. Incorrect instructions can make a cell cease
functioning normally and even give it the chance to develop
cancer.

Type Of Gene That Cause Cancer

Proto-oncogenes, tumor suppressor genes, and DNA repair
genes are the three primary gene groups that are typically
impacted by the genetic alterations that cause cancer. These
modifications are commonly referred to as cancer's "drivers."

Proto-oncogenes play a role in regular cell division and
proliferation. However, these genes may develop into cancercausing genes (or oncogenes), allowing cells to grow and survive
when they shouldn't by being changed in specific ways or being
more active than usual.
Genes that decrease tumors are also involved in regulating

cell division and proliferation. Certain tumor suppressor gene
mutations can cause cells to divide uncontrollably.

DNA damage must be repaired using DNA repair genes. It
is common for cells with mutations in these genes to also
have mutations in other genes and chromosomal abnormalities
including duplications and deletions of chromosomal segments.

These alterations might work together to turn the cells malignant. Scientists have discovered that specific mutations frequently
occur in a variety of cancer forms as they learn more about the
molecular alterations that cause cancer.

There are numerous cancer medicines on the market right

now that focus on cancer-related gene alterations. No matter where the cancer first developed, several of these treatments are available to anyone with a tumour that carries the targeted mutation.

Difference Between Cancer Cells & Normal Cells

In many respects, cancer cells are different from healthy ones.
Cancer cells, for instance:

1: Develop despite without receiving commands to do so.
Only when they get such signals do normal cells expand.

2: Ignore signals that typically instruct cells to halt their
division or undergo apoptosis, often known as programmed
cell death.

3: Infiltrate adjacent regions before moving on to other body
parts. Most normal cells do not travel across the body and cease

growing when they come into contact with other cells.

4: Instructing blood arteries to expand toward malignancies.

5: These blood veins transport waste from tumors and
provide oxygen and nutrition to the tumors. The immune
system normally eliminates damaged or abnormal cells.

6: Fool the immune system into sustaining and promoting
the growth of cancer cells. As an illustration, certain cancer
cells persuade immune cells to defend the tumor rather than
fight it.

7: Acquire many chromosome alterations, including as

chromosome component duplications and deletions. Some cancer cells contain twice as many chromosomes as healthy cells do.

8: Depend on different nutrients than healthy cells do.
Additionally, as opposed to most normal cells, certain cancer cells use a distinct process to produce energy from nutrients.
This promotes the rapid growth of cancer cells.

9: The aberrant actions that cancer cells frequently exhibit are essential to their survival. This fact has been used by researchers, who have created treatments that focus on the aberrant characteristics of cancer cells. For instance, certain cancer treatments stop blood vessels from directing their growth toward tumors, thereby depriving the tumor of the nutrients it requires.

Chapter 5: When Cancer Spreads

Metastatic cancer is a type of cancer that has progressed from
the site of its initial formation to another location in the body.

Metastasis is the process through which cancer cells spread to
other areas of the body.

The initial or original cancer's name and cancer cell type also apply to metastatic cancer. For instance, breast cancer that spreads to the lung and develops a tumor is considered
metastatic breast cancer rather than lung cancer.

Metastatic cancer cells typically resemble the original tumour's cells when viewed under a microscope.

Additionally, there are some biological similarities between metastatic cancer cells and the initial cancer cells, such as the presence of particular chromosome alterations.

People with metastatic cancer may occasionally live longer with the aid of treatment. In other circumstances, preventing the spread of the cancer or reducing the symptoms it is causing are the main objectives of treatment for metastatic cancer. Most

cancer patients die from metastatic disease, which can seriously

impair how the body works.

Tissue Changes That Are Not Cancer

Cancer is not always a result of tissue changes in the body.
However, if some tissue alterations are not treated, they may
progress to cancer. Here are a few instances of tissue alterations
that are not cancer but are occasionally under observation in
case they develop into cancer.

When cells within a tissue expand more quickly than is typical,
an accumulation of extra cells is called hyperplasia. Under
a microscope, the tissue's cells and organizational structure
nonetheless appear normal.

Numerous causes or factors,

including prolonged inflammation, can lead to hyperplasia.
In comparison to hyperplasia, dysplasia is a more advanced
disorder. There is also an accumulation of extra cells in
dysplasia.

However, the tissue's organization has changed, and the cells appear aberrant. Generally speaking, the likelihood of developing cancer increases with how aberrant the cells
and tissue appear. Some forms of dysplasia could require
monitoring or treatment, while others don't. An aberrant mole
that develops on the skin and is referred to as a dysplastic nevus is an illustration of dysplasia. While most dysplastic nevi do not progress to melanoma, some do.

The condition that is considerably further advanced is carcinoma in situ. The aberrant cells do not infect the surrounding tissue the way cancer cells do, despite the fact that it is commonly referred to as stage 0 cancer. However, certain in situ carcinomas may progress to malignancy, thus they are typically treated.

Type Of Cancer

More than 100 different cancers exist. Typically, cancer types are called for the organs or tissues in which they first appear. For instance, brain cancer begins in the brain and lung cancer begins in the lung. The type of cell that gave rise to a cancer, such as an epithelial cell or a squamous cell, can also be used to describe the condition.

Here are several cancer forms that start in particular cell types:

Carcinoma

The most prevalent kind of cancer is carcinoma. Epithelial cells, which are the cells that line the interior and exterior surfaces of the body, are responsible for their formation.

Epithelial cells come in a variety of varieties, and when they are magnified under a microscope, they frequently resemble columns.

There are distinct names for cancers that start in several types of epithelial cells:

Adenocarcinoma

Adenocarcinoma is a type of cancer that develops in mucosa or fluid-producing epithelial cells. Occasionally, glandular tissues are referred to as epithelial tissues. Adenocarcinomas make up the majority of cases of breast, colon, and prostate cancer.

The basal (base) layer of the epidermis, which is a person's
outer layer of skin, is where basal cell carcinoma, a type of
cancer, first appears.

Squamous cells, which are epithelial cells found just below
the skin's surface, are where squamous cell carcinoma develops.
Numerous other organs, such as the stomach, intestines, lungs,
the bladder, and kidneys, are lined by squamous cells. Squamous
cells appear flat under a microscope, similar to fish scales.
Epidermoid carcinomas are another name for squamous cell
carcinomas.

The epithelial tissue known as transitional epithelium, or
urothelium, is where transitional cell carcinoma, a type of cancer, develops. The linings of the

bladder, ureters, renal pelvis, and a few other organs are made up of this tissue, which is composed of numerous layers of ectoderm cells that can
develop bigger and smaller. Transitional cell carcinomas are
a type of cancer that can develop in the bladder, ureters, or
kidneys.

Sarcoma

Sarcomas are tumors that develop in the muscle, fat, blood
vessels, lymphatic vessels, and fibrous tissue that make up soft
tissues and bone (such as tendons and ligaments).

The most typical type of bone cancer is osteosarcoma. Liposarcoma, Kaposi sarcoma, malignant fibrous histiocytoma, liposarcoma, and dermatofibrosarcoma protuberans are the most prevalent varieties of soft tissue sarcoma.

More details can be found on our page on soft tissue sarcoma.

Leukemia

Leukemias are cancers that start in the bone marrow, which produces blood. Solid tumors are not produced by these malignancies. Instead, the bone marrow and blood become overpopulated with aberrant white blood cells (leukemia cells and leukemic blast cells), which drive out healthy blood cells. It may be more difficult for the body to manage bleeding, fight infections, or deliver oxygen to its tissues when the normal blood cell count is low.

There are four common forms of leukemia, which are categorized according to the type of blood cell the malignancy first appears in and if the condition worsens quickly (acute or chronic) (lymphoblastic or myeloid). Leukemia grows more swiftly in its acute forms than in its chronic variants.

Lymphoma

Cancer that starts in lymphocytes is called lymphoma (T cells
or B cells). These white blood cells, which are a component of
the immune system, combat disease. In lymphoma, aberrant
cells accumulate in the body's lymph nodes, lymph arteries, and
other organs.

The two primary kinds of lymphoma are as follows:
Reed-Sternberg cells, which are aberrant lymphocytes, are
present in people with Hodgkin lymphoma. Usually, B cells are
the source of these cells.
Non-Hodgkin lymphoma is a broad category of malignancies

that originate in lymphocytes. The malignancies can develop
from either B or T cells and can spread swiftly or slowly.

Multiple Myeloma

Plasma cells, another type of immune cell, are where multiple
myeloma develops. Myeloma cells, which are aberrant plasma
cells, amass in the bone marrow and develop into tumors in
bones all throughout the body. Kahler disease and plasma cell myeloma are other names for multiple myeloma.

Melanoma

Melanocytes, which are specialized cells that produce
melanin, are where melanomas, a type of cancer, first appear

(the pigment that gives skin its color). The majority of
melanomas develop on the skin, but they can also develop
in other pigmented tissues, such the eye.

Brain and Spinal Cord Tumors

Tumors of the brain and spinal cord can take many distinct
forms. These tumors are given names based on the cell type
in which they originated and the region of the central nervous
system where the tumor first appeared. For instance, astrocytes,
which assist maintain the health of nerve cells in the brain,
are the origin of an astrocytic tumor. Brain tumors may be
malignant (cancer) or benign (not cancer) (cancer).

Other Types of Tumors

Germ Cell Tumors

One sort of tumor that starts in the cells that produce sperm
or eggs is known as a germ cell tumor. These tumors can be
benign or cancerous and can develop practically anywhere on
the body.

Neuroendocrine Tumors

Cells that release hormones into the blood in response to
a signal from the nervous system are the source of neuroendocrine tumors. These tumors can produce a wide range of symptoms because they may produce higher than usual levels
of hormones. Malignant or benign neuroendocrine tumors are
also possible.

Carcinoid Tumors

Neuroendocrine tumors include carcinoid tumors. Typically,
they are slow-growing tumors that affect the digestive system most often in the rectum and small intestine). Carcinoid
tumors can secrete chemicals like serotonin or prostaglandins,
which can lead to carcinoid syndrome. They can also spread to
the liver or other parts of the body

Chapter 6: What Cause Gene Mutations

Gene mutations can happen for a variety of reasons, such as:
genetic changes you are born with.

It's possible that you have an inherited genetic mutation from
your parents. Only a small proportion of tumors are caused by
this kind of mutation.
gene changes that take place after birth.

The majority of gene mutations happen after birth and
are not inherited. Gene mutations can be brought on by a
variety of factors, including smoking, radiation, viruses, cancercausing substances (carcinogens), obesity, hormones, chronic inflammation, and inactivity.

Gene mutations typically take place during healthy cell growth. However, cells have a system in place that may
detect errors and correct them. On occasion, a mistake gets
overlooked. This might result in a cell developing cancer.

What Do Gene Mutations Do

A healthy cell may be instructed by a gene mutation to Permit quick development.

A gene mutation may instruct a cell to divide and develop
more quickly. This results in the creation of numerous additional cells with the same mutation.
failure to inhibit unchecked cell growth.

Normal cells are aware of when to cease growing so that there
are the proper proportions of each type of cell present. Tumor
suppressor genes that tell cells to stop growing are lost in cancer
cells. A tumor suppressor gene mutation permits cancer cells
to keep multiplying and accumulating.

Make blunders when fixing DNA mistakes. DNA repair genes

scan a cell's DNA for faults and correct them. A mutation in
a DNA repair gene may prevent additional errors from being
fixed, resulting in malignant cells.

The majority of cancer mutations are characterized by these changes. However, a variety of additional gene alterations can also result in cancer.

How Do Gene Mutations Interact With Each Other

Gene mutations can happen for a variety of reasons, such as:
genetic changes you are born with.

It's possible that you have an inherited genetic mutation from
your parents. Only a small proportion of tumors are caused by
this kind of mutation. Gene changes that take place after birth.

The majority of gene mutations happen after birth and
are not inherited. Gene mutations can be brought on by a variety of factors, including smoking, radiation, viruses, cancer causing substances (carcinogens), obesity, hormones, chronic inflammation, and inactivity.

Gene mutations typically take place during healthy cell growth. However, cells have a system in place that may
detect errors and correct them. On occasion, a mistake gets
overlooked. This might result in a cell developing cancer.

The gene mutations you're born with and those that you acquire throughout your life work together to cause cancer.

For instance, if you've inherited a genetic mutation that predisposes you to cancer, that doesn't mean you're certain to get cancer. Instead, you may need one or more other gene mutations to cause cancer. Your inherited gene mutation could make you more likely than other people to develop cancer when exposed to a certain cancer-causing substance.

It's not clear just how many mutations must accumulate for

cancer to form. It's likely that this varies among cancer types

Risk factors

The majority of cancers occur in people without any recognized risk factors, despite the fact that doctors have a notion
of what may enhance your risk of developing cancer. Some
elements that are known to raise your risk of cancer include:

Your age

The development of cancer can take decades. The average
age of those who receive a cancer diagnosis is 65 or higher.
Cancer is not just an adult disease, even though older adults are
more likely to develop it. Cancer can be detected at any age.

Your habits

It is well recognized that some lifestyle decisions raise your
risk of developing cancer. Tobacco use, excessive alcohol use
(up to two drinks per day for males and up to one drink per day for women), frequent blistering sunburns, excessive sun exposure, being fat, and unsafe sex are all risk factors for cancer.

Although some habits are easier to modify than others, you
can adjust certain behaviors to reduce your risk of developing
cancer.

Your family history

A very small percentage of cancers are brought on by an inherited disorder. If cancer runs in your family, mutations could be handed down from one generation to the next. If you want to find out if you have inherited mutations that could make you more likely to get a particular cancer, you might be a good candidate for genetic testing. Remember that not everyone who carries an inherited genetic mutation will develop cancer.

Your health conditions

Your risk of getting some types of cancer might significantly
rise if you have certain chronic health conditions, such ulcerative colitis. Discuss your risk with your doctor.

Your environment

Hazardous chemicals in the environment may raise your
risk of developing cancer. If you go places where people are
smoking or if you live with someone who smokes, even if you

don't smoke, you could inhale secondhand smoke. Additionally,
exposure to chemicals like benzene and asbestos at work or
home is linked to a higher chance of developing cancer.

Complications

Cancer complications and their effects on therapy include:

Pain

Even while not all cancers are unpleasant, pain can nonetheless be brought on by the disease or its treatment. Pain brought
on by cancer can be adequately managed with medications and
other methods.

Fatigue

Cancer patients' fatigue might have numerous reasons, but it
is frequently treatable. Although it is frequently transient, fatigue related to chemotherapy or radiation therapy treatments is prevalent.

Trouble breathing

A sense of being out of breath could be brought on by cancer
or cancer treatments. Treatments could provide comfort.

Nausea

Some tumors and cancer therapies might make you feel sick.
If your therapy is likely to make you feel queasy, your doctor may be able to forecast this. You may be able to avoid or lessen nausea with the use of medications and other treatments. Constipation and diarrhea. Your bowels may experience diarrhea or constipation as a result of cancer or cancer therapy.

Loss of weight

Weight loss may result from cancer and cancer treatments.
Cancer robs healthy cells of their nutrition and snatches their
sustenance. This is challenging to treat because it frequently
isn't impacted by calorie intake or the type of food consumed.
Utilizing artificial feed delivered by tubes into the vein or stomach typically has little impact on weight loss.

Alterations in your body's chemistry

Cancer can alter your body's regular chemical balance and raise your risk of life-threatening problems. Chemical imbalances may show symptoms such as excessive thirst, frequent urination, constipation, and confusion.

Brain and nervous system problems

Cancer can irritate neighboring nerves, resulting in pain and a loss of one bodily part's functionality. Headaches and stroke-like symptoms, such as weakness on one side of your body, can be brought on by brain cancer. abnormal immunological responses to malignancy. In some instances, the immune system of the body may target healthy cells in response to the presence of cancer. These extremely unusual reactions, known as paraneoplastic syndromes, can cause a wide range of signs and symptoms, including trouble walking and seizures.

Cancer that spreads: Cancer may "metastasize" (spread to other places of the body) as it gets worse. The type of cancer

determines where it spreads.
Return of cancer: Cancer recurrence is a possibility for cancer survivors.

Some malignancies have a higher recurrence rate than others. Consult your doctor about steps you can
take to lower your chance of developing cancer again. After
your treatment, your doctor might come up with a plan for
your ongoing care. In the months and years following your
treatment, this plan can call for routine scans and examinations
to check for the return of cancer.

Chapter 7: 7 Things To Know About Alcohol & Cancer

The American Cancer Society recently revised their cancer prevention recommendations. One of the suggestions is to abstain from drinking.

While abstaining from alcohol is optimal for preventing cancer, women who choose to drink should limit their intake to one drink per day, while males should limit their intake to two drinks per day.

We discussed the new alcohol guidelines and their implications with Therese Bevers, M.D., medical director of MD Anderson's Cancer Prevention Center.

1: What do you think of these new alcohol policies?

The American Cancer Society's recommendations are now more in line with what is known regarding the relationship between drinking and the risk of developing cancer.

Additionally, they are in line with suggestions made by other institutions like MD Anderson and the American Institute for Cancer Research.

We are aware that alcohol raises the risk of a number of malignancies, including liver and breast cancer, colorectal cancer, esophageal cancer, pharynx and larynx cancer, oral cancer, and pharynx and laryngeal cancer. According to this guideline, drinking less lowers your risk of developing cancer.

2: How does drinking alcohol increase a person's cancer risk?

Alcohol can raise a person's risk of cancer in a variety of ways,
including the following:

Alcoholic beverages contain ethanol, which degrades to
acetaldehyde, a recognized carcinogen. This substance ruins
DNA and prevents our cells from healing the harm. This may
promote the growth of malignant cells.

The levels of hormones like estrogen can be impacted by
alcohol. These hormones serve as transmitters, telling our
cells to multiply and flourish. More cell division increases the
likelihood that something will go wrong and that cancer will
spread.

Alcohol reduces the body's capacity to absorb and break down
a number of crucial nutrients, including the vitamins A, C, D,
and E, as well as folate. These vitamins and minerals shield the
body from cancer.

Alcohol contains worthless calories. Extra calorie intake
can result in weight gain, which raises a person's chance of
developing cancer.

3: If alcohol causes cancer, why do you advocate serving
sizes?

We understand that the majority of Americans won't entirely
give up drinking alcohol. We can therefore provide some
direction on what moderate drinking looks like if they decide

to drink.

It’s crucial to keep in mind that drinking increases your risk of developing cancer. There is no safe level of alcohol, just like there isn’t for cigarettes or processed meat.

4: What information regarding alcohol and cancer should people receiving active cancer therapy know?

The negative effects of chemotherapy and other cancer treatment medications can be made worse by alcohol. These negative consequences consist of oral sores, dehydration, and nausea. Additionally, drinking alcohol raises the possibility of getting cancer again.
Patients with cancer should discuss alcohol consumption with their doctor.

5: How does alcohol consumption impact a person's likelihood of developing cancer again?

Alcohol is a risk factor for several malignancies, according
to studies. The connection between alcohol and cancer recurrence, particularly in those who have finished cancer treatment, is unknown. However, since drinking raises cancer risk, it is advisable to avoid doing so after receiving a cancer diagnosis.

6: How does a person's history of drinking affect their chance
of developing cancer if they stop drinking?

According to research, the chance of developing an alcoholrelated cancer decreases over time once you stop drinking.

Although it might take several years to completely eliminate

that risk, giving up is a crucial first step in enhancing your
health and lowering your risk of developing cancer.

7: What is the best thing to drink if I'm going to have alcohol?

There is no one alcoholic beverage that is superior to another
when it comes to reducing your chance of developing cancer.

All of them contain ethanol, which has been linked to an increased risk of cancer. This includes beer, wine, and liquor.

Choose something with less calories if you want to reduce the effect of alcohol on your waistline. Avoid, for instance, beverages with sweet mixers.

I would look for other strategies to protect my heart health if

I were to drink red wine for that purpose.
According to certain
research, red wine contains substances that are good for the
heart. However, there are numerous ways to maintain heart
health. The benefits of consuming wine may not outweigh the
risk of cancer.

Symptoms Of Cancer

Depending on what region of the body is affected, cancer can
create a variety of signs and symptoms.

The following are some typical indications and symptoms of
cancer that are not particular to this disease:

Fatigue Under the skin, a lump or thickening might be felt.
alterations in weight, such as unplanned loss or increase
Skin alterations such skin that is turning yellow, darkening,
or red, sores that won't heal, or modifications to existing moles
alterations in bowel or bladder patterns.

Persistent cough or breathing issues
Having trouble swallowing
Hoarseness

persistent heartburn or discomfort following a meal
persistent, irrational joint or muscle pain
persistent, irrational fevers or sweats at night
Bruising or bleeding that is not normal.

Prevention

Alcoholic beverages come in a wide variety, but they all have the
potential to be harmful and develop an addiction. In addition
to making people drunk, alcohol permanently harms the liver
and other organs. If you or a loved one is having alcoholism
problems.

There are various ways to lower your chance of developing
cancer, including:

Stop smoking: Quit smoking if you do. Stop smoking if
you don't already. Smoking is associated with more cancers
than just lung cancer. You can lower your future chance of developing cancer by giving up now.

Avoid excessive sun exposure: The sun's harmful ultraviolet
(UV) radiation can raise your risk of developing skin cancer.
Reduce your exposure to the sun by seeking out shade, donning
sunscreen, or donning protective gear.

Eat a healthy diet: Pick a fruit and vegetable-rich diet.
Choose lean proteins and healthful grains. Limit the amount
of processed meats you eat.

Exercise most days of the week: A lower risk of cancer is associated with regular exercise. On most days of the week, try to get in at least 30 minutes of exercise. Start out slowly if you haven't been exercising frequently, and work your way up to
30 minutes or more.

Maintain a healthy weight: Obesity or being overweight may

raise your risk of developing cancer. By combining a nutritious
diet with regular exercise, work to reach and maintain a healthy
weight.

Drink alcohol in moderation: if you decide to indulge. If you
decide to consume alcohol, do so sparingly. That entails up to
one drink per day for women and up to two drinks per day for
males for healthy individuals.

Schedule cancer screening exams:According to your risk
factors, discuss with your doctor which cancer screening tests
are best for you.

Ask your doctor about immunizations: Your risk of cancer is increased by specific viruses. These viruses, such as hepatitis B,

which raises the risk of liver cancer, and human papillomavirus
(HPV), which raises the risk of cervical cancer and other malignancies, may be prevented by immunizations. Consult your
doctor to determine whether you should receive a vaccination
against these viruses.

Summary

Drinking alcohol is associated with the risk of several cancers, with the data confirming that alcohol may cause, or at least be involved in causing, seven specific types of cancer. Alcohol is carcinogenic and is one of the avoidable risk factors.

We think it's important to educate consumers about the dangers of alcohol consumption, but we also want to make sure that this is done thoroughly, methodically, and without dramatizing or trivializing the facts.

Drinking is typically associated with the pursuit of pleasure sensations and is frequently thought of as a special treat on occasion. Any claims on the danger of developing cancer must be understood in that light.

More specifically, it is necessary to

acknowledge the link between alcohol use and the chance of
contracting cancer. while also taking the overall risk of various
malignancies into account.

For less common malignancies, such oropharyngeal or laryngeal cancer, the dose-effect relationship is stronger; for more prevalent diseases, like colorectal cancer, it is weaker.

Cancer may also manifest as a result of a combination of various external carcinogenic substances and one's own genetic
makeup agents. These substances could be biological (viral, bacterial,
or parasitic diseases), physical (ultraviolet radiation), or both
alcohol) or chemical (including ionizing radiation).

Alcohol use and cancer risk should be related, not acknowledged while keeping in mind that there isn't a single cause for
cancer.

Finally, any recommendations with regard to drinking and
health must be made in light of epidemiological data and
evidence for all diseases known to be caused, in part, by alcohol.

This obviously includes cancer, but also includes other diseases,
such as diabetes, pancreatitis and cardiovascular diseases. With
regard to the latter, significant data has shown that, compared
to those who do not drink alcohol, people who drink excessively
increase their risk of coronary disease, but people who drink
moderately reduce that risk.

Health is a complex matter that cannot be reduced to a single concern about whether or not one is likely to develop cancer.
For those who are concerned solely about cancer prevention, given what is currently known, it is recommended that drinking be reduced as much as possible.

For everyone else, following the low-risk drinking guidelines remains a very reasonable choice. As we have been saying for years, moderation is always in good taste.

About The Author

Relationship expert Dr. MARC REGAN is a philosopher who focuses on behavioral and addiction difficulties.

He worked with thousands of customers in government-funded services before switching to full-time writing. His writing is supported by scientific research and his practical expertise.

He is the author of the books 21st century women, 16 fertility food to increase fertility & make pregnancy easier, oneitis the reason for your obsession with romance, mood tracker & The most effective weapon for relationship & self-improvement are Made of small stuff

Printed in Great Britain
by Amazon

46459126R00056